THE HERO FROM
NITHDALE STATION

The remarkable true life story of
Major Charles W.H. Tripp — "The Boss"

DICK TRIPP

Written by Dick Tripp
E: dick.tripp@christianity.co.nz
www.christianity.co.nz
© 2019 Dick Tripp

Published by
Wild Side Publishing
wildsidepublishing.com

This is a work of non-fiction. A limited edition was previously published:
Stories of My Mother and Father
August 2018
ISBN 9-780-473-450854

This book is copyright. Except for the purpose of fair review, no part may be stored or transmitted in any form or by any means, electronic or mechanical, including recording or storage in any information retrieval system, without permission in writing from the publishers. No reproduction may be made, whether by photocopying or by any other means, unless a licence has been obtained from the publisher or its agent.

The Daily Telegraph excerpt, *The Boss*, from *The Second Book of Obituaries; Heroes and Adventurers*, was used with permission from Dawn O'Driscoll, Syndication Account Manager, The Telegraph, 27 November, 2018.

Cataloguing in Publication Data:
Title: The Hero from Nithdale Station
ISBN: 978-0-473-46229-1 (pbk.)
ISBN: 978-0-473-46230-7 (ePub)
Subjects: Biography, Pioneer farming, Stories of Southland, New Zealand Non-Fiction, New Zealand History, World War II

Cover design by Janet Curle,
Wild Side Design wildsidedesign.net

Manuscript, text layout and proofreading by Sally Tripp.

First printing 2019 yourbooks.co.nz
International distribution Ingram Spark

Acknowledgements

My thanks go to the late Phillip Klap whose encouragement motivated me to get started on this book.

I am grateful to those who have shared stories of my parents: Joe Studholme, Ginger and Raema Redman, Frank Williams, David Bosomworth, Katrine Brown, also my sister Rosa Peacock and her husband Graham for helpful suggestions, stories and for checking the manuscript. The Waiouru War Museum provided details of my father's award. Margaret Pullar gave helpful editorial comments and early proofreading.

Finally, my gratitude goes to my wife Sally, who, together with her friend Rosemary Koller, spent many hours in final proof reading. Also to Sally for her computer and layout skills, and preparation of the photos for publication—without her help the project would probably not have got off the ground.

Endorsements

A more enjoyable glimpse into the life and times of one of this community's cornerstone families I haven't ever experienced.

Charlie and Myra Tripp of 'Nithdale' have left a legacy like few others, and the story of the pivotal role family, farm and community played in that legacy has been superbly told by their younger son Dick.

This is a very human story of vision, determination, humour and focus, through both peacetime and war, highlighting the role of human potential to overcome trying circumstances, be they foe on distant shores or rabbits and gorse on the home front.

An easy read and a valuable slice of life from days past.

Tracy Hicks, Gore District Mayor

This book fills in the picture of pioneer families in rural New Zealand, which prepared them for even greater things at home and abroad. Major Charles Tripp (both Silver Star and DSO for the same service) led Fijian and Tongan commandos in dangerous situations to inform American troops in the Solomon Islands, and Dick's mother was awarded a QSM for her community work. This book will ensure that these stories will not be forgotten.

Rt. Rev. Henry Paltridge, former Bishop of ACK Meru in Kenya

My grateful thanks to you, Dick, for sharing the stories of your father and mother and for taking those moments in time to ask the questions which enabled you to re-tell their stories to us now and the generations to follow.

The memories of your father Charlie Tripp; a man of high moral values, tempered with frugality and abundant generosity, a man who would not ask anyone to do something that he would not or could not do himself, a man inspired by others, who in turn was an inspiration to those that knew and served with him.

This book is a great read, and whilst Charlie is no longer with us, he and his story can still act as a great role model for people today.

Rev. Bruce Cavanagh, Padre, Gore District Memorial R.S.A.

My father, Mac Tulloch, spent time at war in the Pacific about the same time as Charlie Tripp. I recall my Dad speaking very fondly of him. He respected him and esteemed him highly.

It has therefore, been a pleasure to read this book and enjoy the stories told here.

I know that all future generations of this family will treasure their recorded history along with those of us fortunate enough to read this book.

What better way do we have to learn other than from those who have gone before us.

Ian (Inky) Tulloch, former Mayor of Gore District

A slim yet most readable and revealing insight into lives of the scions of a pioneering New Zealand family. Whether farming in Southland or fighting in the South Pacific, these are real people, real places, real action.

Bishop Brian Carrell

Contents

Foreword 7

My Father 11

Cambridge University 14

The Farm 16

My Mother 20

My Maternal Grandparents 26

My Paternal Grandparents 33

War Stories 44

Back Home 66

Appendix 73

About the Author 79

Foreword

What an interesting and unique book this is! It combines two things that New Zealand readers love: tales of how our back country was tamed, and action adventures of our modest war-heroes. This book has them both as it recounts stories ranging from the lives of early settlers on our South Island sheep-farms through to military action in the South Pacific.

Readers will want to thank the author both for preserving these memories and making them available in a memorable way. Dick Tripp is blessed with the ability to recall vivid details of the lives both of his father and his equally notable mother—and other assorted characters—in a cascade of anecdotes. Today's mostly urban Kiwis will warm to these tales – some of them with a laugh-out-loud quality as well.

In re-telling history that threatens to evaporate away as the memory of its characters fades, nothing beats well-told stories. In this book we meet rabbits and frugality, the great depression and early motoring, desperate fighting in the Pacific theatre and the little-known history of Fijian, Tongan and other Pasifika Commandos with their New Zealand officers, especially Charles Tripp, the resourceful, courageous (and almost accidental) 'hero of Nithdale.'

Dr Bob Robinson, Laidlaw College

Charlie Tripp

Myra Tripp

Stories of My Father and Mother

My Father

My father was a remarkable person, with his high moral standards, legendary fitness, personal discipline, visual memory, powers of observation and leadership qualities. However, rather than present a detailed account of his character and gifts, I intend simply to tell stories as they come to mind. Many of them were told to me by my father himself when we were doing things together, and some by others who knew him. Some I gathered from the book *Pacific Commandos* by Colin Larson, published in 1946 and now well out of print though available in libraries. Most of the details about the early farm days are culled out of Mother's booklet *Memories of Charlie W. H. Tripp*. Most of the stories of life at Glenaray are from Barbara Harper's book *Eight Daughters and Three Sons* and George Pinckney's eulogy at Cara Unwin's funeral. Mother was also a woman of unique qualities. Needless to say, my parents had a considerable influence on my life and I have always considered it a great privilege to have been their son.

My early years were always tinged with awe of my father. One of the lessons I gained from him was the importance of daily exercise for one's general wellbeing. Father's fitness was legendary. He was a great walker. Even at Christ's College he was known for this. When they went for their annual hike up Rapaki Track on the Port Hills, rather than take the bus to the bottom of the track, as the rest of the school did, he would walk all the way from the College and then back afterwards. (I did this one year to prove I could do it too!) In his last year, he won the Mile Walk, an athletic event, which they unfortunately don't have today.

When sailing through the Panama Canal in a steamship on his way to Cambridge University, Father helped the crew in the engine room for a week or two, stoking the boilers on a four-hour shift.

When at Cambridge he met J. P. Muller, Physical Instructor to the Royal Family, at his Institute of Physical Training in London. Muller was the author of *My System*, fifteen minutes of daily exercises designed to use every muscle in the body a little every day and to keep supple around the joints. Muller was a Dane who was born with a heart problem and not expected to live. However, he did live, and developed this series of exercises. During his lifetime he won 134 prizes, of which 125 were Championship and First prizes, and only nine Second prizes, in almost every possible branch of sport and athletics. Father encouraged me to do these exercises and I have done some of them all my life. It has paid off. I still have copies of the books *My System* and *My System for Ladies* by J. P. Muller, and at least the first can be read free on the internet.

I remember Father telling me about walking with his dogs from Orari Gorge to Timaru (30 miles) and calling in at his old school, Waihi, on the way. When he bought Nithdale farm, 11 miles from Gore, in 1924, it was covered in vast areas of gorse and broom. He joined the rugby club, and after work he would walk the eleven miles into Gore for the weekly practice. To save a couple of miles he would wade or swim the Mataura River, and after practice walk home. At 40, he was the second oldest member of the Commandos in the Pacific, but he could outwalk any man in the unit.

Father was always a very early riser. He would get up at five most days, have his cold bath, do his Muller's exercises and, in early days, feed his hack, and if time allowed grub some gorse before breakfast. I have always got up around six o'clock. I cannot remember a single instance in my life when I was out of bed before Father, and that was even in the last two years of his life. He would usually be in the kitchen having a cup of tea and reading the paper when I got up. My sister Rosa told me that towards the end of his life she managed to persuade him to stay in bed until 7 o'clock one morning. He confessed that he felt a little better for doing it.

Joe Studholme told me that shortly after his marriage to Sue they paid a visit to Nithdale. Father asked him the night before if he wanted him to knock on his door at 6.30am so they could have an early breakfast and Joe could come down with him to check on the men for their jobs for the day. Joe would have liked to have slept in a little, but thought he should be considerate, so said "Yes". Father took him down to the shed and discovered that they were a bit short of fencing materials for the day's work, so asked Joe if he would come into Gore with him to see the stock agent to get more supplies. When they got to Gore the store was still shut as it was about eight o'clock, before opening time. Father said he knew where the agent lived so took Joe round to his house and knocked on the door. The man answered the door and thought it was a bit early—he was still having his breakfast. However, he went to the store and got Father what he wanted. Driving home, a short distance from Gore Father made the remark, "You know, if the Japanese invaded New Zealand, Gore would fall before breakfast as they would all still be in bed".

There were two events in the year that meant much to Father—the annual bull sale, when he could catch up with many friends who would come for the occasion, and the annual Commando reunion, which he would never miss. On one occasion a friend was staying with Father two nights before the sale. Without any warning, Father knocked at his door at 5.30 am to inform him that he had run his bath and cooked his breakfast of two poached eggs, and that he would take him to look around the bulls at 6 o'clock.

When he first went to Nithdale, the bathroom was separate from the rest of the house, and often the taps would freeze in winter. He would run the bath the night before and would then have to break the ice before having his bath in the morning. Mother, who was raised on Glenaray Station, together with 10 brothers and sisters, said they always kept a hammer in the bathroom for that purpose.

Cambridge University

When Father was at Cambridge he rowed at number seven in the first Trinity Hall boat. We have an oar he won for getting four bumps in the 1923 May Inter-College races, and the bow of another boat, which he won when a boat he coached got the four bumps. The oar hangs, with the oar that his father won in the fourth Trinity Hall boat, in the hall at Orari Gorge.

Harold Abrahams, who took part in the 1924 Olympics with Eric Liddell, and whose story was told in the film *Chariots of Fire*, was at Cambridge at the same time as Father. Father told me that when they had the Inter-College athletic competitions the rowing club took part, as Trinity Hall didn't have any great athletes. During the long jump Abrahams didn't bother to turn up for the first two jumps, but did during the third and final jumps. As his jump was three feet ahead of the others, that was all that was required. In the 120 yard hurdles he didn't bother to take his jacket off. Father, who was second, said that when he got to the finishing line Abrahams had taken his jacket off and hung it on a post before Father had finished. However, Father beat him at the high jump. For some reason that was something Abrahams was not good at. Father told me that when he came back from the war he could kick the lintel at the top of the door in our sitting room — the lintel was higher than him.

I was with Father the night he died. The nurse came in and asked him what he wanted for tea. He asked for a cup of soup and some jelly. When the jelly was served, there were four slices of banana on top. As he ate the jelly, he told me that when he rowed for his college at Cambridge he experimented to see what was the best food to eat before a race. He found that banana was not good to row on, and that the best thing was two poached eggs on toast two hours before the race. As he was telling me this, he pushed the four slices of banana to the edge of the plate and didn't eat them. My sister Edith and I left the hospital to return to the farm at 9 pm and said we would be back in the morning. However, the hospital rang about midnight to say that he was unconscious and they couldn't wake him. We returned to the hospital and I was with him when he stopped breathing about 2 am. I think that the reason he didn't eat the banana was because he knew the The Big Race lay ahead. He died at 89, but I don't know how long he would have lived if he hadn't smoked in his younger days—lung cancer finally caught up with him.

The friends he made were a highlight of his time at Trinity Hall, Cambridge. He was on the same floor as a Mr. Thomas (who worked with Lord Rutherford) and they often had bournvita together before bed when Thomas would talk about what they had been doing in the laboratory that day. Father studied in partnership with John Oates in the Agriculture Course. John was the brother of Captain Oates, who sacrificed his life on the way back from the South Pole to give Scott and the others a better chance of making it back to base. John had been a major with a DSO at a very young age in the First World War. Father asked me to look him up when in England, which I did. Father also got to know John Hammond well. He was a junior animal science graduate, who was a great help to younger students, and later became famous for his work in artificial insemination.

Father's uncle, Leonard Tripp, was also a Trinity Hall man and was a friend of Sir Earnest Shackelton. While Shackelton was in England he invited Leonard to see over the "*Quest*" before the ship sailed for the Antarctic. He took Father with him, and Shackelton showed them all over the ship and introduced them to some of his men, including Frank Wild. This was the trip on which Shackelton died. He was buried in South Georgia. Leonard also took Father to see the model farm in Sussex of Mr. Rowett, who had financed the expedition, as well as the Rowett Institute for research in animal nutrition in Scotland. After Cambridge, Father travelled back to New Zealand via Canada, having some interesting experiences on the way, which are described in Mother's book *Memories of Charlie W. H. Tripp*.

The Farm

Father had several jobs before purchasing Nithdale. His first was at Pyne, Gould & Guiness. He took the place of his cousin Tom Hope, a stock agent, for the busy season, as Tom had broken a leg. This was a useful experience for a farmer-to-be. He then went down to Glenaray in the autumn of 1923 where he assisted with the sowing of lime, did some fencing, stacked peat at the Blue Lake, joined in the muster of 18,000 sheep from the Titans, and joined the rabbiting team, dropping pollard poison from the Blue Mountain and Basin Creek camps.

In 1924, he taught at Waihi for six weeks to fill in after the headmaster Joe Orford died. Following this, he went to work in his father's office at Tripp & Rolleston in Timaru, where he was shown how to write legal letters and other work done by law clerks. This only lasted a few weeks, as in August he heard from Dalgety's in Gore that there was a 3,444-acre farm called Nithdale for sale near Gore. One of the reasons he chose not to work at Orari Gorge was because Arthur Blackiston, who was managing the farm for the family, told him that, as he was family, he would only be paid half wages. Father had sent soil samples from the Gorge to Cambridge to have them analysed to see if the application of lime was needed. Only half the amount he recommended was put on the land, but this wasn't sufficient to obtain the desired result.

Nithdale had been purchased by James Scott in 1875 and named after his home on the river Nith in Dumfriedshire, Scotland. Before he sold to Father, he had bought another 230 acres from Fred Trapski and 180 acres from Todd who owned what had been the Otaraia Hotel on the Old Coach Road. These additions increased the size of Nithdale and they are now named Trapskis and Todds blocks.

Father asked his uncle, George Pinckney, to look over Nithdale with his father and Jim Reynolds, Dalgety's agent. I remember Jim visiting on several occasions to check stock, and drinking tea with him in the kitchen, so he must have been around for a while, as I was not born until 1932. He was a good friend of Father's. Father was not very interested in the house and only saw the kitchen. The sale was on 1st September 1924. My Father took three and a half days to get from Timaru to Gore in his Model T car, converted to a truck with no hood. On board he had a bed, bedding, saddle and bridle, a desk, suitcases, all-weather gear and two dogs. When travelling in the dark he had to get out and light the kerosene lamps. His dogs had never seen a tram and jumped off the truck and chased one down George and Princes Streets in Dunedin. Eventually he caught them at the Post Office. Father did not know the value of stock, so asked George Pinckney to bid for 900 ewes, 8 draft horses, 1 hack, 30 cattle of mixed breeds, including a cow to be milked, and 32 wethers for mutton, at a local sale.

He first employed a married couple in the house and a teamster, but the couple didn't stay long as the man thought the work was too hard. Albie and Mrs. Murdoch had been in the top cottage since 1923. Much time was spent turning the big red tussocks into fallow land, which took a lot of discing and harrowing with a six-horse team to break down until it was suitable for sowing grass.

Father named various paddocks and cottages through the centre of the farm after the Cambridge rowing course on the river Cam—First Post, Corner, Ditton Corner, Grassy Corner, Station, Bridge and one other. There were masses of gorse hedges that had got out of control, having spread from the original sod walls. A neighbour at Burkes Hill quoted his relationship with the previous owner, James Scott, as so friendly that they did not even need a boundary fence between them. There were rabbits everywhere. Father's sister Margaret visited Nithdale several months after he had bought it. The view from Trapskis was far from inspiring—run-down brown-top paddocks, falling-down fences, rabbits everywhere and gorse down to the homestead. She told her Canterbury friends that the best thing about the place was that there was a river where you could drown yourself.

Father would take pot shots at rabbits from his bedroom window in the morning before they ran into the trees. There were 21,000 rabbits taken off Nithdale the year before Father arrived. Harry Redman, with help from his brother Harvey and son Ginger, who was then 15, poisoned 18,000 while Father was away fighting in WWII. I remember going out and seeing Harry sitting beside a great pile of them and skinning them. I did skin a few myself. Ginger worked for Father from his teenage years and eventually became farm manager, ably supported by his wife Raema.

If I shot or trapped rabbits I would skin and dry them stretched on wire, and when in Gore I could get a shilling each for them. When Edwin Wilding bought his farm near Ohai in 1923 it was over-run with rabbits, like the rest of Southland. In his first year he did the rabbiting and employed a man to do the farm work. That year he made 600 pounds. Father employed a rabbiter and did the farm work himself, with a teamster—and made nothing. The Pukerau Rabbit Board began operation in 1946 with Harry as its foreman and they did a good job of keeping rabbit numbers down. Father told me how, in later years, if he saw a single rabbit in a line of trees, he would ring the Board and a man would come out from Gore with his dogs and be sure to get it. Sally and I usually visit the farm for a couple of weeks a year, but I have only seen one rabbit on Nithdale in recent years and no gorse bushes.

An amusing, though tragic story that Father told me, concerned a man of German origin who came to work in the district. He was an eccentric, and offended some of his neighbours by working out in the paddocks in the nude. He was as brown as a berry. One day he got into an argument with a local publican. He told the publican, that if you wrote out a cheque, and then died before it was cashed, the recipient would not be able to cash it. The publican was certain it could be cashed. The fellow then bought a bottle of whiskey for which he paid a cheque. He went home, drank the whiskey, fell into a local pool and drowned. The publican discovered he was not able to cash the cheque.

Father was always very frugal. In 1927 his father visited and brought a wireless, two more chairs and a vacuum cleaner. Father thought this very extravagant. He never thought buildings and furniture were worth spending a lot of money on, as they didn't make money. The sitting-room had a small fireplace, shabby wallpaper and lino on the floor. He added his desk, a table, two basket chairs and an armchair he had bought for two and sixpence. I think this was the one he sat in for the rest of his days. He oiled his boots in one corner, while a 16 gauge shotgun, a .22 rifle, a .38 rifle, a fishing rod and oddments stood in other corners. When Edwin Wilding came to visit in 1927 he still had only one bed, so they tossed up for it. Edwin won, so Father slept on the floor on a mattress. Basil Unwin worked on Nithdale for two years in 1926-27. When he came to visit in 1929, after Father had married, the sitting room had a new stone fireplace. The room had been papered and carpeted, and now had furniture and a few pictures on the walls. As he walked into the room he exclaimed, *"Oh Myra, you have ruined this room!"*

My Mother

Father often visited Glenaray in his Model T Ford. On 31 October 1928 he married Myra, fifth daughter of George and Edith Pinckney of Glenaray, at the Woodbury Church. Afterwards there was a reception at Orari Gorge. George had purchased Glenaray with his two brothers-in-law, Jack and Bernard, in 1898. Edith was a daughter of Charles Tripp, so Mother and Father were first cousins. They went to Franz Josef Glacier for their honeymoon. Coming home to Nithdale they motored from Timaru in a Standard car that my Grandfather no longer used.

Mother was a good farming partner for Father. She had spent much of her days on horseback, out mustering with the men, rabbiting, or just riding with her sisters. She and her siblings were trained to muster and draft sheep and, by way of diversion, ferreted and skinned countless rabbits, caught eels and mice, and trapped and roasted sparrows and starlings. A plate of roast sparrows would be kept for their father's dinner. All the girls could whistle like shepherds. She told me that if they found a rabbit hole with young rabbits in it, they would dig them out, line them up and cut their heads off with a spade. There is a framed photo on the wall at Orari Gorge of the Pinckney girls lined up on their horses with dozens of rabbit skins. One hundred was the record.

On one occasion, when mustering up in the mountains, one of the men got lost in a snowstorm. His remains were found three years later by several of the girls who were out helping with the mustering. He was curled around a tree. They reported it to the police who brought him back in a kerosene box. Mother was out riding with others in the area later and they decided to see if they could find the spot. They found a knucklebone, took it back to school and asked the teacher if she knew what it was. On one occasion the musterers turned up at one of the outback huts and all they could find to eat was some cheese. One of them wrote the following ditty:

I've mustered in the Southern Alps:
I've shorn in a Union shed:
I've climbed Glenorchy's rocky heights:
I've slept in a spear-grass bed:
I've tuckered in the roughest joints,
And seen the whiskey freeze,
But never have I mustered yet
On half a pound of cheese.

Mother was very generous. She would often drop veges from her garden or baking in to staff or neighbours and would visit new folk who moved into the district. She read regularly to residents of a retirement home in Gore. She was in the 1982 Queen's Birthday Honours List, receiving a Queens Service Medal for her work in the community and in particular, I believe, for her work with the Kaiwera Women's Institute, of which she was a founding member, and chairperson for many years. She was also actively involved with the Plunket and Red Cross. This award meant a lot to her.

On a vacation from Cambridge one year, I took two weeks to hitchhike around Holland, Germany, Switzerland and France. In Germany, I visited a displaced persons' camp near Hamburg. People, who had been brought from the East by the Nazis during the war to work in their factories, were still there 10 years later. When I told Mother about conditions there, she regularly corresponded with a lady who helped there, and sent gifts, blankets I believe. It was the same when she was at Orari Gorge, when she would regularly drop in gifts of fruit, veges or meat to staff and friends.

Mother stressed the importance of a good diet. A nickname I received at Waihi Primary School was 'Brown Bread'. All the other boys had white bread, but she insisted that they give me brown bread. Health was an issue. On occasions, when at the beach, she would line us up and get us to gargle with seawater. Mother inherited a great faith in the food value of onions. The Pinckneys had friends in Waikaia with a common interest—children and health. Mr. Taylor was bank manager there. They had 21 children. During the early 1900s there was an outbreak of diphtheria in Waikaia, and though there were Taylor children in every class at the school, not one of them got the disease. The doctor questioned Mrs. Taylor about this, but the only reason she could give for her children's health was to say, "onions every day". During the winter, each child had to eat one onion every day. Mother credited onions for the fact that during the worldwide flu epidemic in the following decade, none of the Pinckneys succumbed.

Ginger and Raema Redman shared stories of my parents' driving skills. Mother never sat a driving test until she reached the age when you had to be re-tested at seventy. Father had spoken to the local traffic officer in Gore in the early days and told him she could drive, so the officer wrote out a licence for her. She tended to make up her own rules. On one occasion she went through a stop sign in Gore and hit a taxi. She made her way to Ginger and Raema, who were living in Gore at the time, and said to Raema, "I think I've done something silly. Do you have a brandy in the house?". On another occasion, she took the corner sharply at the T junction where the old letter box used to be and hit another car. She made her way across the paddock to Ginger and Raema and asked Ginger if he would go and sort it out while she and Raema had a brandy.

Father took Ginger on one occasion to look at a raised board in a woolshed. Ginger offered to drive on the way home, but Dad insisted on driving. Taking a short cut on a gravel road Dad overshot a corner. Ginger said they were airborne and ended in a paddock down a bank. Father continued driving around the paddock, got up speed, and got up the bank. They drove for a mile or so with neither of them saying a word. Then Father stopped the car and said, "I think we both need a drink". He reached into the glove box and got a flask of whiskey and a small glass. As the glass was a little dirty he got out a hanky, which Ginger said was just as dirty, and wiped around the top of the glass. They both had a drink. When Father was getting old, and a local spotted him on the road to Gore, Ginger said the man would send a warning message to his friends that Charlie Tripp was on the way to Gore.

As Mother liked riding better than housework, she helped Father with mustering, drafting, etc. He told me that on one occasion, working together, they got the record for dipping 1,000 sheep in a day. He would push them into the long dip and she would push them under with a crutch. The swim dip was used until 1947. The first wheel tractor was bought in 1932 and later a crawler, though a six-horse team of draught horses was used until the late forties. Lime sowing started on Nithdale in 1924 when lime was 25 shillings a ton. As soon as financially possible, 500 tons was sown every year and right through the slump, when it was ten shillings a ton.

The depression years were difficult. W. D. Hunt, Chairman of Wright Stephenson, agreed to help any of his clients financially, as long as they kept on spreading lime. Even so it was difficult. Ewes were sold at the Gore sale at ten to forty shillings a full pen. Steers could be bought or sold for three or four pounds a head. From 1929 on, wool, which had been 18 pence a pound, went down to six and even three pence a pound. In 1932, a Kaiwera farmer got six pence each for his lambs, and one shilling each for his rabbit skins. When Glamis Cottage was built for Watty Gunn and his wife in 1933, it cost 300 pounds. A bedroom added after the war cost 600 pounds. During the depression, people would ride out from Gore and spend the day grubbing gorse and broom, merely for the sake of a meal. The stumps were used for firewood.

Because of the importance of lime for the land, Father was instrumental during the depression years, together with Erskine Bowmar, George Pinckney and H. M. Copeland, in establishing two limeworks, one in Southland, and the Victory Lime Works at Mt. Somers. These men were all on the Board of Directors. He also purchased, with others, a butcher's shop in Gore during the depression. As they could not afford sufficient staff they cut up the meat themselves. Father learnt a lot about beef in the process. Father was also instrumental in the decision to found the Alliance Freezing Works. The decision to go ahead was made in his sitting room in the early hours of the morning after a lengthy meeting.

Father was very involved in the local community—the rugby club, scouts, RSA, aero club and local hall committees, where his quiet and firm personality was appreciated and respected.

Father was known for his honesty. Someone told me that he was present at an auction, when Father was selling some of his bulls. They came to one of the last to be sold and the auctioneer got to a certain price, but couldn't get another bid. He turned to Father and asked if he would like to say a word about the bull in hope of getting a higher bid. Father said that he didn't think the bull was a particularly good one and probably wasn't worth the price that had already been offered! Another disarming habit he had was to assess a discussion on livestock matters when opinions were thrown around quickly among fellow farmers and breeders. Sometimes, when the discussion had switched to another topic, he would suddenly, out of the blue, rekindle the earlier discussion with a deeply considered opinion of the previous topic. It was usually close to the mark. His attention to detail was evidenced in the collection of pelvic cavity bones stored on top of the dog kennels. He had collected these cavities from cow carcasses and could recall the calving history of each one to indicate its ease or problem at calving. He kept his tools in first class order and sharpened his own. If I remember rightly he said he had been shown that skill by a butcher in London.

Soon after the war started, all the men on Nithdale enlisted, including Bill Cousins, Watty Gunn, Ken Worthington, Hughie Roy, Mic O'Hagan, Albie Murdoch and Father. Albie was not accepted because of his age, so stayed on to manage the farm. Sadly, Ken was killed in action on Crete, but the others made it home. Albie was a great fisherman. He would take me fishing in the Kaiwera Stream. He used a dry fly and told me to strike the moment the fish shut its mouth, otherwise it would be too late. I did not realise at that stage that I suffered from astigmatism, so I could never see the fish coming.

Father was well known around New Zealand for his Polled Hereford Stud. He was one of the first to recognise the value of the Polled species. He got his first Hereford calves in the 1930s and his first Polled Hereford Bull, Ajax, after the war, from F. E. Humphreys, who had already established a stud in the North Island. Ajax had a quiet temperament. We have a picture of Rosa and Leonard sitting on his back. In 1975, after Rosa married Graham Peacock, an English farmer in North Yorkshire, Father sent two bulls and 14 females for her to establish a stud over there. Four years later, one of the stud sold for the record price of 11,000 guineas and was also Supreme Champion at the Edinburgh Hereford Sale. This bull went on to become United Kingdom Sire of the Year in 1982/1983 and two of his sons were purchased by the Milk Marketing Board for their A1 stations in the United Kingdom.

My Maternal Grandparents

My Grandfather, George Pinckney, went to school at Radley, England and then to Oxford University. He was no scholar, but did very well at rowing and athletics. He had come out to New Zealand against his father's wishes, with a letter of introduction to Charles Tripp, to work on Orari Gorge, as he didn't like working inside in his father's bank in Salisbury. Charles was very satisfied with his progress in farming and wrote to his father in glowing terms saying, "You should be very proud of your son." George fell in love with Edith and wrote home to his family, "I've met a girl I'm going to marry when she is old enough." Barbara Harper writes in *Eight Daughters and Three Sons:*

> Though only fifteen years of age, Edith was socially mature. Being the youngest of a family of four boys and four girls, educated at home by governesses and living in a house frequented by relatives and friends, she was well equipped to approach her contemporaries and elders with ease and confidence. She didn't suffer from the self-consciousness and gaucheness of an adolescent girl coming home from boarding school. She was extraordinarily uninhibited for a child of the Victorian era and took pleasure in shocking her older sisters by her remarks and actions, daring to leap on a horse astride. Fair, blue-eyed, slim and vivacious, no wonder she appealed to the rather sombre George.

George purchased a farm of 300 acres just seven miles from Orari Gorge and while there, asked Edith to marry him. When she told her parents, they were speechless, especially her father who had expected George to approach him first. The result was that they were not allowed to see each other for six months and were given permission to write, but only twice. Edith was taken to Christchurch to enjoy the social scene. She attended many balls and parties, but soon discovered that none of her partners could waltz as beautifully as George. When she returned home, the only means of contact with George was secret messages conveyed by Jim Maling, a cousin of Edith's, who was working for George on his farm. Maling said he had never worked harder in his life. Every morning George called at his bedroom door, "It's five o'clock Jim. I'm making the porridge". At the age of 21 she was finally allowed to get married. George was twenty-eight. They were married by Bishop Harper, Edith's grandfather, at the Woodbury Anglican Church on 8 June 1893 with the reception at Orari Gorge. Later that afternoon George was seen milking his cow at the back gate of his farm.

It wasn't a good year financially for marriage, with sheep prices at one shilling a head, the price of a haircut. Edith learned to cut George's hair, so saved him 12 shillings that year. He couldn't pay her the £25 annual allowance that was expected of him. "Prices will rise. They can't be like this always," Edith would say optimistically. "You mustn't worry George." And she would add the remark she was to make so often to her children in later years, "We must count our blessings". *Count Your Blessings* was to become my Mother's favourite hymn.

I spent two years, when I was five and six, at Glenaray with my cousin, Basil Unwin, who was the same age. We had a governess. My memories of Grandfather were that he was a little eccentric. He was not a conversationalist. Apparently he was not allowed to speak at the table when young until he was seventeen. When George was at Oxford, my paternal grandfather, Howard Tripp, was at Trinity Hall, Cambridge. After his first meeting with George he remarked what an extraordinarily quiet chap he was. "He only seemed to have one topic of conversation—rowing." I can't ever remember him talking at the dinner table though I understand he enjoyed the chatter, which could get rather boisterous in the evenings when they had all had a glass of cider from a keg in the hall. He never told his children to be quiet. He was, however, renowned for his yelling and swearing in the sheep and cattle yards. The only time I remember him talking to me was on an occasion when he sat me on his knee, examined my fingernails and asked me if I bit them. I probably did, but wasn't going to admit it. He had some unorthodox ideas. From the age of six his children were not allowed milk or tea until they were 12, but they could drink beer or cider. This may well have been because back in England it was known that water and milk could cause plague and illness. Not much was known about bugs in those days.

There was a story in the family that George had never tasted water until he arrived in New Zealand, not even at Radley, where they always had a mug of beer at lunchtime. He was quite happy for the children to have a glass of cider or beer in the evening. He had utter disgust for anyone who took too much and couldn't behave themselves after a drink. The children didn't have cake, and were supposed to eat fruit between meals, and were not given meat except on Sundays until they were twelve. However, they made good friends with the cook at the staff cookhouse from whom they got lumps of cold meat and buns. A salad of shredded lettuce was served with every lunch and dinner. The children broke the rules whenever opportunities arose, mainly on market days. George was a stickler for time, particularly for meals. If he wanted a meal at a special hour, it would be at an odd time like eight minutes past 12, or 11 minutes to six. There was a biscuit tin of blackballs and a case of walnuts to munch in the evenings for every school holiday.

When oysters were in season he would buy a sack of them in the shell. The family and visitors opened them, and as they had to be eaten within two days, they were eaten raw or made into soup. He carried the prices of all his purchases in his head, and Edith then wrote the cost down in her notebook. He had great concentration and could draft several thousand sheep in a day, working three gates in front and one behind, and seldom make a mistake. He still had time to curse the shepherds and cadets for not keeping the sheep up to him or for not keeping the dogs quiet at the back. He was a generous man. When shopping he would bring back boxes of fruit and vegetables, when reasonably priced, and drop them off at the gates of his workers, especially the married ones.

When the children were small, they were always encouraged to go barefoot, and when older, in boots or low heels. They were clad simply, often scantily. George hated high-heeled shoes. When sitting by the fire one night he asked Cara (his youngest daughter) if he could look at one of the shoes she was wearing. When she handed it to him he took it onto the veranda and chopped the high heel off with an axe. The daughters knew their father's attitude toward makeup, so when returning home from the races, or some social event, lipstick was wiped off at Gore. Sweets were anathema to George. On a trip to England with their first two children, Jack and Hilda, in 1899, he was indignant if other passengers offered them sweets. He had notices attached to their backs, PLEASE DO NOT GIVE ME SWEETS. He did the same on the return trip.

Although they led an outdoor life, Edith made sure that her daughters didn't lose their femininity. She taught them to sew and knit, and she read to them a lot. They always changed into frocks in the evening for dinner. They were never allowed to wear shorts, and no trousers were allowed on Sundays. I don't have strong memories of Edith other than that she was a gentle person. She was described by one of her cooks as the kindest and wisest person she had met. She was always calm and boundlessly considerate and hospitable, and loved by the station staff. "Never raise your voice to a child," was one of her favourite sayings. One lady, who often worked at the homestead, said she was the only person she had known who never raised her voice at anyone, no matter how much she was provoked. Other favourite sayings which often punctuated the conversation were; "Don't get stuck, children, try some other way," or "Life is all in the state of mind." Her favourite was "Count your blessings." She was no disciplinarian, and had a horror of the 'don't' approach. She was greatly loved by her daughters' friends, many of whom visited

Glenaray, and she astounded them by the way in which she remembered their individual tastes. She had an unfailing sense of humour.

George never liked his children going away, and if it hadn't been for their mother the girls felt they would never have gone to school. He had a phobia about his children becoming 'booky', and had no hesitation in calling them away from their lessons to help with drafting or dipping. He would give a special whistle, Morse Code K, (long short long), which was their party line phone number, wherever the children were, or whatever they were doing. They obeyed the call with delight, closed their books and were off. They all learned to count sheep when very young. It had to be raining very hard before the children stayed inside for long. If their father found them sitting around the fire, when he considered they should be outside, he would pour a jug of water on the fire.

In summer they slept in two large tents, as he thought it was healthier for them to sleep outside. He used to say, "You only need to learn to read and write and do arithmetic." When he heard that Bindy was given four marks for French in his matriculate exam, he said, "Quite enough too." The matron of St. Hilda's remarked that the Pinckney girls were like little wild goats straight off the tussocks, until they learned to accept the restrictions of civilised life. When Hilda left school, WWI was on and there was a shortage of labour, so she had to work very hard in the house and on the station. She wanted to learn to drive the car, and her father agreed provided she never travelled over 25 miles per hour.

George was in England when his father died of blood-poisoning. An operation couldn't save him. However, George was convinced that it was the operation that had killed him, and when he returned to his family, he made Edith promise never to allow anyone to operate on him. Edith kept dried puff balls in the house for treating wounds and this was found to be effective. When asked by Dr. Unwin, "Weren't you afraid of blood-poisoning?" she replied, "I have never heard of blood-poisoning." Raw meat on wounds was another effective remedy. George's cure for all ills was a Turkish bath. George became renowned—or notorious—for his cures. When Edith was in Dunedin giving birth to Cara, a measles epidemic hit Glenaray. Eleven of the 13 persons in the homestead had measles, including George. He used to smoke, and to avoid catching them he smoked harder than ever. He was so annoyed when he did catch them that he never smoked again. When he contracted rheumatic fever, he refused to take the aspirins the doctor prescribed for him but accepted Edith's usual cure—hot packs.

George and Edith drove a buggy to a monthly Anglican Service in Waikaia. A monthly Presbyterian service was held in the Glenaray dining room, and later in the school building at Gow's Creek. Edith played for the Presbyterian services for 25 years. Edith was elected as Country Queen for the 1917 Queen Carnival in Gore. George had tried hard to persuade her not to stand, as he was terrified he would have to appear and speak in public himself.

George started putting lime on the paddocks in 1906. When asked by one of his daughters years later, "When is the best time to spread lime?" he replied, "Whenever you have a minute to spare and a penny to spend."

After World War I, the government decided to split up some of the larger properties to provide farms for returning servicemen. They sent three agents to Glenaray to see if the station would be suitable for division. George got four of his daughters (including Mother) to take them for a ride to look at the property. He instructed them to take the agents through some manuka scrub and boggy ground on one of the roughest parts of the station. To the girls' silent delight, the three men appeared very nervous and led their horses far more than was necessary. The story goes that when they got back, the men, who were not used to riding, had to eat their dinner off the mantelpiece. When they gave their report, they stated that the place was not suitable for splitting up! George was to become recognised as one of New Zealand's most able high-country farm managers. I understand that Glenaray is today the largest privately-owned sheep station in New Zealand.

The following poem is one I wrote in memory of Mother for the 100th anniversary celebration of Glenaray Station. It may give some idea of what it was like growing up in the Pinckney family at Glenaray. It is based on Kipling's poem *IF*, which I grew up with, as it was framed over the loo in the bathroom at Nithdale:

IF

(Dedicated to Mother)

If you can keep your cool when all around you
Are organising you against your will,
Imposing rules and manners that confound you,
And yet maintain your sense of humour still.
If you can keep your elbows off the table,
Until you reach the age of twenty-one;
If you fancy neat the Hokonui label,
Or gargle at the seaside just for fun.

If you can run your bath the night before,
And break the ice before you take the plunge;
If you can eat an onion in the raw,
And yet decide to not throw in the sponge;
Or bath in "Pinckney Puddle" without cringing
Which Hope has filled each week with water cold,
Or take cod liver oil without whingeing,
And thumb your nose at doctors, yet grow old

Or scoff a can of worms to spite your sisters,
Or keep your hams and cheeses till they crawl,
Or put up with raw meat upon your blisters,
Or mind toadstools on your scratches not at all.

If you can make a heap of all your boodle
And risk it on a Glaxo share or two,
And then just watch it increase while you doodle,
And grow to bless a generation new.

If you can ride from dawn till evening lingers,
And muster on a loaf of bread and cheese,
Or give a piercing whistle through your fingers
To call your dog from half a mile up-breeze.
If you can open oysters by the sackful,
When Father's weekly trip to Gore is made,
Or curse your dogs with swear-words by the packful,
Or decapitate wee bunnies with a spade.

If you can give a lead in your community,
And pioneer groups for tasks that are well done,
For building friendships, fostering local unity,
And get a QSM, sincerely won.
If you can fill your days with good activity,
With acts of kindness, which you love to do—
Then you are blessed and honoured in our memory,
And maybe yet you'll make a Pinckney true.

My Paternal Grandparents

One thing I regret is not asking Father to tell me more about his father, Charles Howard Tripp, generally known as Howard, who founded *Tripp & Rolleston*, solicitors in Timaru. I don't remember Howard, as he died when I was four years old. However, Father did tell me two stories about him worth recording. Howard was out pig hunting at Orari Gorge on one occasion when he got charged by a large boar. He climbed a tree to escape and got up it with his gun, but in doing so he dropped his bullets. The gun was a muzzle-loader—you put the powder in and then add the pellets in the barrel. He searched his pockets and fished out a small pocketknife. He opened the blade and shot the pig with that.

My grandfather was a keen astronomer. I inherited a sextant and an altimeter which must have belonged to him. He possessed a telescope which he gave to Christ's College and which was used in a small observatory at the top of School House for many years. It has now been updated with a more modern one. There had been several shipwrecks along the Timaru coast. Captains had said that they were puzzled by that, as they were following the map and hadn't known they were so close to the shore. However, the maps were originally surveyed by Captain Cook and hadn't been upgraded. My grandfather wondered whether they were accurate, so decided to do a check. He did his own survey. Father told me he used a bucket of water to get the angle of the sun. Normally it was correct procedure to use mercury, as it would provide a more accurate reading. Grandfather estimated that the map put the coast about a mile out from where it should have been. He wrote to the Admiralty in London and they sent out someone to do a check. They found that he was only 11 feet out in his calculations!

My grandfather is credited with buying the first car in South Canterbury. It was built in Timaru by Cecil Wood, who is credited with being the first man in New Zealand to fit an engine to a bicycle. The car was a three-wheeled vehicle, built to carry two people, with a two-horsepower motor, belt driven to the right wheel only, tiller steering, travelled 10 miles an hour and weighed 500 lbs, not unlike Henry Ford's first invention. It tended to pull to the left. What is known is that Howard and Ruby set off from Timaru to drive to Orari Gorge, a journey of 30 miles with a lack of bridges and good roads. It took three days. On the second night they parked the vehicle, walked to Tripp Settlement, and came back to retrieve the car next day. A replica of the car was made and taken up to Orari Gorge for an event at which we could take rides in it around the front lawn.

My cousin, Jenny Coutts, passed on a story told her by her Aunt Margaret, which took place when Howard was on a visit to England. He had purchased a car there and was travelling to York with his daughter Rosa (Jenny's mother). Apparently they got a puncture when nearing York. Rosa got out and said she would walk on ahead and Howard could pick her up when he had fixed the tyre. He fixed the tyre and drove on to York. When he arrived he realised he had passed Rosa without noticing.

The only people from Howard's generation whom I knew were Uncle Leonard and Aunt Katie. Aunt Katie spent her last years at Orari Gorge and was there when we were living in the Tin Hut (a cottage nearby). Rosemary Thomson, who was a little older than me, came over from Peel Forest occasionally to stay. She taught me to tickle fish. On one occasion she took me up the creek from the Tin Hut to the Homestead and we must have caught 10 or so. I took them in on a string to show Aunt Katie, who was sitting in the smoking room. She was horrified. Rosa told me of an occasion when she was young and staying at the Gorge. Dan and John Pinckney were there, and Uncle Leonard was also visiting. He was a great environmentalist. Dan and John showed Rosa how to tickle a fish, and then persuaded her, in her innocence, to take it in on her finger and show Leonard. Mother saw her going in and tried to stop her, but she wasn't quick enough. Leonard saw it and was very annoyed. He made a rule there was to be no fishing either side of the bridge. As Rosa was innocent, Mrs. Graham cooked it for Rosa's tea, but John and Dan were not allowed any.

There were two magnificent gums on the bank above the house, which were a great nuisance as the leaves blocked the gutters. This meant hours of work. Leonard would never let them be cut down in his lifetime. Rosa told me that on one occasion Mother had said to Katie that, because they darkened the house, she didn't think the Lord would want them to stay. Her reply was, "I'll tell you what; I am expecting to meet him before you do, so when I do I will ask him."

I only have one memory of my Father's mother, Ruby (nee Laidlaw). She had ill health in her later years and died in 1945, when I was 12 years old. When living in Timaru with Mother for a short time, when Father was at the war, I visited her, and remember her sitting up in bed looking frail. Ruby was from Galashields, Scotland, and Howard had met her on board ship when returning from a visit to England. They were engaged within a week and married in 1900. In *Kettle on the Fuchsia* Barbara Harper says she was an elegant, charming, gentle person and became much loved in Timaru and among her South Canterbury friends.

Trinity Hall 1st May Boat, 1923
Bumped Christ's 1, Queens 1, Lady Margaret 1, Caius 1 over the four races.
Father is number 7, leading the left-side rowers

The Crew

Bow. E G Saunders   4. R A Pearson   7. C W H Tripp
2. H Boulton   5. J D Monro   Str. F G G Cox
3. G H Bell   6. A J Dix Perkin   Cox. J D Brown
Coach. Col G L Thomson

Myra, Tom Hope, Kathleen (Mother's sister)
Horses: Commodore, Piebald, Cairo, Duntroon

Father and Mother's wedding at Woodbury, 31 October 1928

Father, Mother
Howard, Edith, Rosa, Dick at Rosa's baptism

Mother, with Leonard and Rosa on Ajax

Charlie and his trusty companion, Joe the dog

Howard, Edith, Dick
Mother, Leonard, Father, Rosa
on the lawn at Nithdale

Father in his favourite chair

Colonel J. H. Nankivell, Military Attache at the United States Delegation, talking with Major C. W. H. Tripp, D.S.O. and Captain D. Williams, M.C. after presenting them with the American Silver Star at Burnham Camp, 17. 8. 1944

Margaret Tripp, Barbara (Margaret's daughter), Father, Mother, Sally Tripp, at Mother's investiture with the Queen's Service Medal

Christ's College Chapel, sketched by Father when he was at school

Howard and Ruby Tripp, 1903, on their first run o Orari Gorge from Timaru.
Two horsepower motor, belt driven to right wheel, tiller steering, speed of 10 miles
per hour, weighing 500 lbs, and built for two

War Stories

Fiji

My father's leadership qualities really came to the fore during his time with the Commandos in the Pacific. He felt it necessary to resist the Japanese and wanted to play his part. In the first year of the war, 1939, he had tried to join the Expeditionary Force, but being 38 and having a family of three, he was over the limit for overseas service (unless as a senior officer). As an alternative, he joined the Southland Regiment. After training in Addington, Burnham, Forbury and Trentham, he was sent to Fiji as a lieutenant. I was nine at the time and living at Orari Gorge, and I remember going out to the Five Hills and looking (as expected, unsuccessfully) for a bayonet that one of Father's unit had lost in manoeuvres on the property. Father's initial job in Fiji was a desk one, as Staff Captain of the 8th Brigade, which didn't appeal to him. He took six months to growl his way out of it, though when he was later asked to set up the Commandos, he found that what he had learned of Army administration was most useful. While in Fiji, he wrote a letter to Mother in which he said that if the Japanese landed in New Zealand, she should take us children to Andrew's Hut, a good way up one of the station creeks, and stock up there.

In April 1942, it was decided to set up the Western, Eastern and Southern Commandos, with Father in command of the Southern Commandos. Larsen wrote in *Pacific Commandos*:

> Charles Tripp was a tall, raw-boned man over forty, of the pioneering type. He was affectionately known as the 'Boss' because of his dominant personality and steadfast character. A successful farmer in civilian life, he used practical, common sense ideas in the development of the Commandos. He had a theory that if he placed absolute confidence in the men under his command, the men would do their utmost to live up to the reputation he gave them. Few failed to respond to his leadership.

The Fijians gave him the respect equal to that due to their high-ranking Chiefs. Some platoons had no contact with the others, except by messengers, but the Fijians always knew by 'bush telegraph' when Father was on his way. When he paid a visit, there would be Fijians from work parties in the bush popping up along the track and every village had a 100% turnout to give a welcome. As he passed by, women would be seen dipping a knee and whispering "tangane"—strong man! Discipline was always handled speedily and fairly, which enhanced his mana with both races. Father became firm friends with the paramount Chief, Ratu Sukuna, who was a man in the same mould, with a law degree from Oxford, and who showed a particular interest in the Commando activities. With his ability to meet people of all ranks as equals, Father used his contacts well to further his military knowledge.

The unit began with about 40 New Zealanders, who provided the officers and sergeants, and 200 Fijians. Later they were joined by some Tongans and Solomon Islanders. The initial idea was that they were to be stationed at various points in the bush around Fiji to delay any Japanese landing until larger forces could arrive. By this time, early in 1941, the Japanese had reached the Solomons and it was generally expected that Fiji would be next in line. When the Commandos eventually joined the Americans in the Solomons, their role was primarily a scouting one, gathering information behind Japanese lines to keep the Americans informed of enemy movements. Father was promoted to captain, and as it was only a small unit of about 300 it wasn't until later in the campaign that he was promoted to major. Someone once told me that if he had been in the Middle East he would have been a general. The Commandos explored their respective areas of some very rugged 200sq. miles, knew every track, river and hill and sorted out places to set ambushes and places for reserves of food supplies and ammunition. The New Zealanders taught the Fijians the use of weapons and military discipline, and the Fijians showed their skills in bushcraft, which were to be so vital later on.

Fitness was a top priority. In training, they would often go until they were exhausted in order to maintain maximum fitness. Dad was impressed with the journey one of his men made right around the main island of Fiji. This meant crossing rivers and going through some of the densest bush and mountainous parts of the island. He told me of one occasion, when in the Solomons, they had to escort a senior American officer some distance through the bush. He was not at all fit. When he wondered how they were going to get their supplies to their destination, he was amazed when Father told him they would be carrying them on their backs. They had to carry most of his equipment, and he perspired so much in the heat that every so often they had to stop and boil the billy to give him a cup of tea. Generally speaking, the Japanese were better fighters in the bush than the Americans, but none of them were as well trained as the Commandos. During their time in Fiji, the unit regularly took on groups of Americans to give them training. One aspect of their training was to be able to move silently in the bush. Father told me that it became so natural to move silently that he often wondered how they did it.

The Fijians were particularly good in the bush and had great eyesight. On one occasion in the Solomons, Dad was walking in front of a Fijian and they started to cross a stream on a log. The Fijian suddenly pulled him back. He had spotted someone at some distance. It took Father a while to see the man as just the side of his face was showing from behind a tree. They stalked him and found it was an American who had slipped out of camp to write a letter home. They sent him back!

On one occasion during their training in Fiji, they decided to set up a mock attack on an American camp. The Americans had taken over the defence of Fiji in July 1942. They were told they would be attacked during the night and so were well prepared. The Fijians went right through the camp during the night. In the morning, one American who was on guard duty found a chalk cross on his water bottle that had been strapped to his waist. Father was not personally involved in the exercise and was talking to an officer in the camp in a tent at one point. When they turned around they noticed a piece of cardboard on the ground on which was written 'Time Bomb'. Not one Fijian was spotted.

An amusing event that Father shared with me that had nothing to do with the Commando training is worth repeating. A Fijian chief presented Dad with a large pig. The Fijian method of killing a pig was rather brutal, so Dad decided he would show them a more civilised way. We always kept a pig on the farm to keep us supplied with bacon. When the time came to kill it, Father would lie it on the ground and cut its throat to let it bleed. To test whether it was dead or not he would touch its eyelid with his knife. If there was no movement, he would know it was dead. He would then place it in a tub of boiling water, which would enable him to scrape off all its hair. To teach the Fijians the civilised way of doing things he had a tub of water heated with a fire under it, and then proceeded to cut the pig's throat. Having touched its eyelid to make sure the creature was dead, he had it placed in the tub. All of a sudden there was a great squeal and a splash, and the pig jumped out of the tub and took off at top speed. However, it only got about 50 yards before collapsing. A little embarrassing! Someone composed the following poem:

One morning in September, as you will all remember,
A pig was caught and killed at C.H.Q.
The company surrounded, were not at least astounded,
By the job they thought the boss could easily do.
A scaffold was erected, and the bath was soon collected—
The only time the bath's been ever used.

The pig had ceased its kicking, its eyelids were not flicking.
And from its throat the blood no longer oozed.
But our confidence was shattered, and our personnel soon scattered,
When in boiling water pig we tried to lay.
(You can tell a kava boozer, by the method that he chooses,)
'Cos the pig got up and quickly ran away.

The Fijians have a hierarchical culture and tended to have a subservient nature and much respect for authority, but Father worked hard to develop a culture in the Commandos in which anyone who had information, suggestions, or wanted to know something could feel comfortable in approaching a senior officer. They wanted self-reliant scouts who could take initiative when necessary. The *Guerrilla Gazette*, a four-page magazine that helped to keep up morale in the unit, reserved the right to poke fun at anyone, irrespective of rank. The editor's favourite joke was to suggest that Father was getting too old for the Commandos and his early morning 'daily dozen' often provoked satirical comment. The joke was all the more pointed because he could outclass anyone in the unit for endurance. Those who boxed with him could vouch for the strength in his arms.

Guadalcanal

After the American Navy's victory in the Battle of the Coral Sea (May 1942), which was a turning point of the Pacific war, Fiji gradually faded into the background. This meant that the Commandos had no immediate objective for training and they began to slacken off a little. Father desperately tried to get his men into action. Eventually, Sir Philip Mitchell, Governor of Fiji, who had taken a great interest in the Commandos, persuaded the Commander of the South Pacific to try out a sample force. At the beginning of December, a Special Party of 30 Commandos was selected from the Southern and Eastern units and sent to Guadalcanal under the command of David Williams. The

Americans at this point were holding a ten-mile beachhead that extended two miles inland and encompassed the Henderson airfield. The job given the Commandos was to patrol beyond the perimeter and provide the Americans with information as to Japanese movements.

Frank Williams was the youngest member of the Commandos, joining up when only twenty-one. He told me that Father felt a special responsibility to look out for him. Frank was included in this initial Special Party and told me of one event in which he was involved. He and four Fijians were leading an American infantry company in the bush, and Frank and two of the Fijians were well out in front, acting as scouts. They suddenly stopped as they sensed that there were Japanese ahead. Father once told me that the Japanese had a distinctive smell and that you could sometimes sense their presence for that reason. However, that may not have been so in this case. There were three Japanese officers hiding behind a large Banyan tree and the scouts noticed that the ground had been trampled around the tree. The Japanese carried swords—this was customary for their officers. If the patrol had continued, they may have had their heads chopped off. A battle started around the tree, which had large roots. A grenade landed at Frank's feet but fortunately there was a root between it and him. He told me he lay flat and put his hands over his head. A Japanese poked his head up to take a shot at him, but one of the Fijians, who had been wounded in his left forefinger but was still holding his gun at his hip, got in first and blew his head off. Frank decided to jump clear of the tree and rely on accurate shooting, which he did, but his gun misfired. A bullet grazed his forearm, but he got back behind the tree. He reloaded and tried again and this time shot a Japanese who was charging at him with his sabre. Frank tried throwing a grenade, but they were on a slope, and it rolled down the hill. The last Japanese finally took off down the hill. When he was about 20 yards away, both Fijians fired. It was found on inspection that both bullets had entered his head an inch apart. Though Frank had a few minor splinters from the grenade, he insisted on staying with his Fijians until they returned three days later with a great deal of information. Frank never fired another shot in action. There were opportunities to ambush Japanese, but the scouts' job was to gather information without the enemy discovering their presence. Frank was later given the Silver Star by the Americans. Of the six Silver Stars awarded to New Zealanders during World War Two, three were given to the Commandos.

The First Commando Fiji Guerrillas

Because the above action was so successful, the Americans requested more Commandos from Fiji. In January, Father was asked to form the First Commando Fiji Guerrillas, selecting men from the Eastern and Southern Commandos, and to be prepared to move to the Solomons at very short notice. As a minimum standard of fitness, he laid down the following; they had to be able to travel for eight hours over rough country and be fit to fight at the end of it, they had to score 20 out of 25 every time with a rifle on the 25-yard range, swim 30 yards in clothes and boots with haversack and rifle and they had to be proficient at unarmed defence and bush-craft. The swimming was a problem for those who had not learned to swim breaststroke, but the New Zealanders struggled through it, even if they had to use two dried coconuts as water-wings. This was permitted, as coconuts are found near most streams in the tropics.

The Fiji Guerrillas were joined by 28 Tongans, carefully selected from the whole Tongan Defence Force. By March, the men were so fit that a five-day test was held for the movement of the entire unit. The men covered over 100 miles of rough, trackless jungle, carrying all their rations, arms and equipment on their backs. One reporter stated, "When the Fiji Commandos raid at night, death wears velvet gloves." Another, after seeing the men on both the assault course and a short manoeuvre, summed up his impressions: "United Nations military leaders have at their disposal hundreds of fighting men, who, through heredity and training, are better qualified to drive the Nipponese from their South Pacific jungle defences than any troops in the field." One of the Fijians requested leave to get married at the last minute. He was a good man and Father didn't want to risk leaving him behind, so reluctantly gave in to his pleading and gave him 48 hours to get the deed done. The man left at dawn one day, travelled over 30 rugged miles to where his bride lived, and returned on the evening of the second day after a wedding and a honeymoon.

Guadalcanal

The convoy left Suva for Guadalcanal on 15th April 1943. Father told me that before they left he approached one of the senior officers and asked that each of his men be issued with a spare pair of boots. You can't fight without boots, and in the wet bush boots had a limited life. The Commandos had found that New Zealand-made boots were better quality than the American, which often had rubber soles rather than leather, and that they lasted longer if hobnails were hammered into the soles. The officer told him not to bother, as boots would be sent up immediately if required in action. However, as soon as he got on the boat, Father, using his own judgement, drafted out an order for two spare pairs of boots for every man and sent it off. Six months later these boots arrived in the Solomon Islands!

When they reached Guadalcanal, the Commandos were detailed to unload the cargo from the holds, and the First Battalion had the responsibility of placing it in dumps on the beach. The captain hoped this would be done before the Japanese bombers paid their nightly visit. It was done in the record time of four hours, much to his relief. He wrote a special letter to the commander of the Fiji Brigade, which is worth quoting in full:

> These troops proved to be the finest that we have had the pleasure of carrying at any time since we have been in the South Pacific area. Their excellent spirit was an inspiration to all hands. Their standard of cleanliness, both as to person and living spaces, was the highest we have encountered. The attitude of officers and their manner of dealing with the men set an example that was freely discussed by the American officers, both Army and Navy, and the results obtained spoke most fluently of the excellent manner in which they dealt with their men. Their keen interest in the individual trooper bore fruit in the spirit engendered in each man. During the unloading at our destination, troops and officers alike made a game of it, and set a record for unloading that will probably stand for a good long time. Prior to this unloading we thought we had made a record, but your forces boosted the tonnage per hour unloaded by almost thirty per cent, thereby giving us something which we will be shooting at for a long time.

Father told me that it was on this exercise that Ben Masefield lost his pistol. He took off his pistol and holster and laid them on a barrel so he could work faster, but when he returned at the end they were gone. There was no time to do a search so he gave the captain the pistol's serial number. Sadly Ben was killed in action, but after the war had ended the pistol was returned to Ben's family in Australia. The captain must have traced it down. The Special Party joined the First Commando Fiji Guerillas under Father's command, with David Williams as second-in-command.

While in Guadalcanal, one Commando patrol, which was on reconnaissance in the mountains behind Henderson Field, had a grandstand view of the greatest air battle fought over Guadalcanal. The Japanese sent a large force of bombers and fighters to attack the airfield from several directions. It was a field day for the Americans, and Zeros (Japanese fighters) could be seen floating down from 20,000 feet by the dozen. The Americans estimated that they had shot down 107 Japanese planes with the loss of only six of their own.

Father told me of another event later in the war when he was on a beach and witnessed another dog-fight. It was at a time when the Japanese were getting desperate and sent 37 bombers over without fighter escort. Though these bombers were able to do quite a bit of damage, the Americans shot them all down. Father saw seven planes going down in smoke at the same time. It was late in June when Dad was officially advised to prepare half of his unit for an attack on New Georgia in the Solomon Islands.

New Georgia

On 24th June the Commandos were given an operation order to prepare for an assault on New Georgia under the command of U.S 43rd Division. Half of the Commandos were to go in the initial attack and the balance to remain in reserve. Later they were to serve under the 37th and 25th Divisions, as each one relieved the other. In the operation order, the unit was referred to as the South Pacific Scouts. The Americans did not relate to the 'Commando' name and did not want any confusion among their troops. The Commandos were happy with this and thought it more fitting to their expected role. They comprised 47 New Zealanders, 1 British, 152 Fijians and 28 Tongans, and attached were 2 British Officers from the Colonial Service and 24 Solomon Islanders.

The initial plan was to capture the Munda Airfield within 10 days, although it was to take 35 days. The Commandos were to patrol from the right flank to the Munda Field, behind Japanese lines, and keep the Americans informed of any outflanking attempt on the part of the enemy. As the New Zealand Commandos used maps to greater advantage than any other infantry unit (the Fijians were not as used to map reading) the Americans supplied them with the latest hastily prepared terrain and photo maps. The New Zealanders studied these until they had a complete picture of the Munda area in their minds. The initial party, which embarked on 2nd July, comprised 23 New Zealanders, 2 Englishmen, 17 Tongans, 87 Fijians and 1 Solomon Islander. They carried all their equipment on their persons.

Father shared with me some of the rules they developed when they got into action. The NCOs and officers always walked in front when on patrol. If the group had information that was useful to the Americans, and one of their number was wounded, they were to leave him behind, as providing information was the first priority. Each man carried three grenades, one of which was kept for himself in case he was captured. This was because of the way the Japanese were known to treat their captives. He told me of one experience when a Tongan was hit by something on the back of the neck and rendered unconscious. When he woke up he found six or seven Japanese standing around him. They had taken all his clothes off him and were obviously curious as to his dark skin. Maybe they wanted to see if he was that colour all over. They asked if he was Japanese or American, and when he said he was Tongan, one of the Japanese took a hip shot at him, which fortunately missed. He saw a gap, which he ran through as fast as he could into the undergrowth. Further shots missed. He turned up at headquarters at dawn dressed in a few jungle leaves.

The Americans tended to go forward behind a blaze of firepower, just shooting at anything, and counted on firepower to get them through, whereas the Commandos were trained to shoot only when they had something to shoot at, and their silence would often baffle the Japanese. The Commandos found that about 15 men was the most suitable number for a fighting unit in the bush, though patrols were smaller, usually at least four. In addition to daytime patrols the Commandos helped man the perimeter defences at night.

The Japanese would often creep close to the American camp at night and scream to frighten them into shooting at, or knifing, each other.

Occasionally they would jump into a foxhole with a knife. Father told me of one occasion when he noticed two Americans with knife wounds in the line-up to the medical unit. He spoke to them and they told him that a Japanese had jumped into the foxhole during the night. Father knew one of his Fijians had been in the foxhole, so sought him out and asked why he had not got the Japanese. His reply was, "No Jap". In their panic they had lashed out at each other. On another occasion an American in the foxhole next to him opened up with his gun. Father asked him what he had seen. He said he saw the head and shoulders of someone in the bush. Soon there was shooting going on everywhere. In the morning Father walked around the camp and found a significant number of dead bush dogs that were responsible for the uproar. Often well-camouflaged, Japanese would hide up trees to take pot-shots at soldiers below. The Commandos accounted for many isolated Japanese snipers. In one early encounter, the Commandos did not realise until morning that some Japanese had slept quite close to them. In taking cover a Tongan and a Japanese dived behind the same tree. The latter asked the Tongan whether he was American or Japanese. He received a lethal answer and his compatriots fled.

One patrol under Ben Masefield set up a bivouac overlooking the Bairoko-Munda trail five miles inside enemy territory from which they supplied information that would give the Americans the key to the whole progress of the campaign.

After Father's death I attended two of the annual reunions of the Commandos. Father would never miss these while alive. At the first of these a toast was proposed to Father in which the speaker told of an event in the battle for the Munda airfield. The Americans were attacking up a slope towards the Japanese, and as the Japanese came down some of the Americans began to panic, and leaving their foxholes, started retreating down the slope. All was a little confused with both Japanese and Americans coming down together. The

Commandos were dug-in in shallow trenches about 30 yards behind the American lines, as they were not primarily a combat unit. Father suddenly stood straight up in his trench and shouted at the top of his voice, "*Get back in your foxholes you bastards!*" Such was his authority that they did just that and the rot was stopped. The speaker also made the comment that Father would never ask his men to do anything he wouldn't do himself. I think it was Frank Williams who told me that the American Generals would treat him as an equal, in spite of his much junior rank. After the war, at a welcome home in the community hall at Kaiwera, I remember a speaker making the remark that Father's men would have followed him to hell!

I remember vividly one day in my young teens when I was in bed, probably with the flu, and Father came in and sat by the bed and started cleaning the pistol he had brought back from the war and which had saved his life on a number of occasions. I got him to tell me the story of his "night out" in a Japanese camp, which he did in some detail and which I remember to this day. He was out on patrol and they came to a path. Father told the others to wait while he crossed the path to make sure there were no Japanese about. There was thick undergrowth on the other side of the path, so he started to run down the path to find a better spot to enter, when suddenly a Japanese opened up with a machine gun. He looked down and saw the Japanese looking over the top of his gun about 10 or 12 yards away. Obviously he had been taken by surprise and had not had time to aim properly, as Father didn't get hit. Father raised his Owen gun to fire, but it jammed, so he threw it at the Japanese to deflect his aim and dived into the bush. The Owen gun was generally a very good weapon for bush fighting and was simple to use. However, sometimes it jammed. Father said that they learned to give the magazine a slap with the hand before firing to prevent this happening. As Father was lying in the bush the Japanese started throwing grenades. One landed right beside him about, two feet away, but he never got a splinter from it. Sometimes the Japanese grenades did not splinter well. He said that the blast practically lifted him off the ground. He thought he had better get out so jumped back on the path and ran back down it, firing his pistol behind him as he did so. He got back to his men and told them to get back in the bush.

He and two Fijians got separated from the rest of the group, and later in the evening they were walking through the bush when suddenly one of the Fijians made a hissing noise to warn Father of danger. Father stopped. He was in a small clearing and a full moon was shining. He did not at first realise it, but he had stopped right beside a foxhole in which were two Japanese. One of them leant out of the foxhole, grabbed Father around the waist and twisted him so he was facing the other Japanese, who placed his gun on the first man's shoulder and fired. Father had his pistol out and shot the first man before the other fired. He still had the magazine of his Owen gun in his pocket. The bullet went though some American money in his pocket, through the dead centre of a small notebook in a leather case, through the metal casing of the magazine of his Owen gun, which he still carried in his pocket, denting some bullets which fortunately didn't explode, and then ricocheted off a cigarette lighter. He got a piece of shrapnel from the bullet in his wrist, which remained there for many years. In his last years, as his arms got thinner, this caused more pain and Rosa took him to Invercargill to have it removed. We still have the notebook, the dented cigarette lighter, the magazine with the hole through it and the dented bullets, in a framed glass case with his medals.

The blast burnt the clothing around his chest and its force knocked Father flat. He told me that he instinctively began feeling for the bullet hole as he went down. He shot the Japanese as he was lying on the ground and scrambled into the bush. One of the Fijians later told him that there was a third Japanese in the foxhole, so the Fijian jumped over Father who was lying on the ground, and hit the Japanese over the head with the butt of his rifle.

The Japanese looked for Father for a while, but eventually gave up. Father was lying behind a log when a Japanese came and lay down on the other side. He waited until he could tell by the man's breathing that he was asleep and then crept away. He decided that the best way out was to pretend to be a Japanese, so he began to walk around normally, and to his relief he found that the Japanese took no notice of him. It worked so well that he decided to look over the enemy positions. He was a bit concerned about his height—Father was a little over six feet and the Japanese were significantly shorter.

At one point, he wasted half an hour stalking a Japanese whom he thought was sleeping in a hollow, but it turned out to be just the moonlight playing tricks. He had thought that if he could get the man's helmet he would look more like a Japanese. Twice a Japanese spoke to him. As he didn't speak Japanese, he thought they might have been swearing at him for disturbing them. He ignored them and continued walking, pausing after a while to make sure he wasn't being followed. At one point he came across a wire, obviously used for sending messages. He usually had a small cutter in his pack, which he had found useful at times, but on this occasion he didn't have it. However, he managed to scrape the insulation off the wire with the edge of the lid of his compass and then twisted the wire until it broke. He came across a small shed in which were bags of rice and some tins of kerosene. He poured some kerosene over the rice. By two or three in the morning he had worked his way through the camp and when he was leaving, he could see Japanese cooking an early breakfast with their canned heat (little tins of fuel that burn without smoke).

After he had left the camp he had one other encounter with the enemy. He heard a Japanese patrol approaching, so lay low while they passed. They had just passed him when, for some unknown reason, one of the group turned and walked straight towards him. He had no choice but to use his pistol again. When he was approaching the American camp later in the morning, he suddenly spotted a Fijian and New Zealander from his group some distance ahead. They spotted him at the same time. The New Zealander thought he was a Japanese and lifted his rifle to fire, but the Fijian knocked it aside and said, "That's Tripp", while Father ducked behind a tree. After the war, Father was having a drink with the New Zealander in a pub and the fellow said to him, "I think I could have got you." Father was able to give the Americans a clear picture of the enemy's position and warned them of the approach of a Japanese patrol for which they laid a successful ambush. With the information, the Americans were soon able to push through to the coast and make the most important beachhead of the operation at Laiana, just three miles from Munda.

Another story that was passed on to the family was from David Bosomworth, a stock agent who knew Father well. It took place when some of the Commandos were landing in a boat on an island. There were Japanese on the beach set up in a concrete structure and firing to prevent any landing. On the boat there was a bulldozer. Father jumped on it, put up the blade to protect himself, and with bullets hitting the blade, drove onto the beach and straight up into the structure. He drove round and round until the Japanese were all buried.

The Commandos had reached a serious state of exhaustion, so most were withdrawn to a spot where they could recuperate, while Father, a sergeant and four Fijians remained at Laiana and another patrol remained with the 169th Regiment. In the meantime, the rest of the Commandos who had been left on Guadalcanal, comprising 14 New

Zealanders, 11 Tongans, 40 Fijians and 23 Solomon Islanders, were sent to join up with the advance group. Wounded Commandos were evacuated.

On one occasion, they were told that a large Japanese force was approaching the Headquarters where the Commandos were stationed. The Commandos manned the perimeter, having given the clerks, drivers, medical orderlies and the like, a very rapid refresher course in small arms. The Command Post was attacked soon after dark, with the Japanese rushing from the jungle from all directions, screaming and yelling. The Commandos' Owen guns mowed them down before any could enter the perimeter. The Fijians could see in the dark better than anyone else, and their shooting was deadly accurate. One of the Fijians in a foxhole was approached by a Japanese officer with a sword in one hand and a grenade in the other. The officer was unable to see the foxhole and was shot when about six feet away. On his person, they found documents giving the full strength of the Japanese force and details of their mission. In the morning the Commandos found 34 dead Japanese bodies that the enemy had been unable to retrieve. American casualties were light and the Commandos were hardly scratched.

Father had numerous small patrols out all over the enemy territory day and night, and the Americans committed hundreds of troops to action on the basis of their reports. Though their job was mainly one of observation, they cut every telephone wire they came across. On at least one occasion, after they had cut some wires, the Americans repaired them and a Japanese interpreter was brought in to listen in to the Japanese conversations.

When American wounded were evacuated they often needed a strongly armed escort, and the Commandos carried out a lot of this escort work and killed many Japanese who tried to ambush them. When in American bivouacs, they also helped to man the perimeters against continued night attacks. The American senior officers were always approachable and co-operative and frequently asked the New Zealanders for suggestions. The New Zealand sergeants often told the American colonels what to 'bloody well do', not realising to whom they were speaking (or pretending not to know). One general held up a conference for an hour, waiting for a New Zealand sergeant to report. American senior officers, including generals, were never too conscious of their ranks to ask for information or advice from any Commando.

It was during this battle that Father received news of his promotion. He had been a Major for a month without knowing it. The Munda Airfield was captured on 5th August 1943. It was estimated that over 3,000 Japanese had been killed and several thousand wounded. Eleven Commandos were killed during the campaign. Sadly, two of their best officers were killed by friendly fire; Ben Masefield by artillery fire and Paul Harper by Americans who thought his patrol were Japanese when they were returning to their camp. Though the Commandos represented only one per cent of the Allied force they probably accounted for over six per cent of the enemy dead in the course of their intelligence work. It was a six-week fight for eight miles of jungle. The strength of the First Commandos was reduced to 11 New Zealanders, 28 Fijians and 6 Tongans. These followed up the retreating enemy and kept them under close observation to the north and west.

After the battle, the commanding general of the 37th Division issued a training memorandum to his forces in which he spoke of 'the non-commissioned officers with the South Pacific Scouts who are white men from New Zealand, and whose capacity for traversing the jungle both by night and by day for many miles, is not equalled by any of our own troops'. Major-General Griswald of the U.S. XIV Corps, which included the 25th, 37th and 43rd Divisions, wrote a letter to the Governor of Fiji in which he stated that the services of the

Commandos were so valuable, and in some instances heroic, as to warrant a special report on their activities. He stated:

> The First Commando Fiji Guerrillas furnished distance reconnaissance patrols, which worked well into the enemy territory, often at great hazard, and furnished battle guides who, in some instances, actually led front line units in combat and assaults on enemy positions. Major Tripp himself engaged in much patrolling in addition to planning, supervising and conducting the activities of the entire detachment in a most capable fashion . . . In addition to Major Tripp, a number of officers, non-commissioned officers and men performed outstanding services characterised by devotion to duty and gallantry."

Major-General R. S. Beisghtler, C. O, 37th U.S. Division, also praised the unit most highly, stating:

> Major Tripp performed services marked by extraordinary fidelity and conspicuous efficiency. He planned the disposition and activities of his small force and conducted their activities to the maximum advantage . . . These services, coupled with Major Tripp's good judgement, knowledge of the area, and knowledge of the enemy proclivities, were a substantial contribution to the security of the command throughout a difficult operation to the successful conclusion of its mission.

Frank Williams, in a talk given at the occasion of the planting of the tree at Orari Gorge in memory of Father, said:

> Memories are of evening discussions with the Boss—be it in a hut, tent, Fijian Bure or under the stars. About the time we were nodding off, he would come forth with a new angle, which would leave us wondering at his knowledge and wisdom. And of course, in happier days, with a bottle of whiskey on the table, he could quote ballads till the cows come home.
>
> He called us by our Christian names in private conversation, at the same time increasing our respect for him.
>
> He lifted our performance, and when anyone achieved something that appealed to him there was just a quiet 'good work', but his eyes would show the depth of his enthusiasm.

Vella Lavella

On 25th August 1943, Father received orders to prepare 50 Commandos to go to Vella Lavella. Two patrols were made up of the fittest men. The sick and wounded were drifting back from the hospitals, but the majority were still weak from the effects of malaria. The party consisted of 10 New Zealanders and 40 Fijians, with four men from the Third N.Z. Division, who went for experience. Father took one patrol with the 35th U.S. Regiment up the east coast, while another, commanded by Captain Williams, was to reconnoitre the enemy position on the northern tip of the island. The patrols were out every day to see if the enemy changed positions, and they carried out some delicate missions close to Japanese positions. A map found on a dead Japanese officer, showed their defensive positions, enabling the artillery to score direct hits on most of the defence posts. The enemy fled leaving much useful equipment behind. The Americans lived on Japanese rations for several days and made good use of their medical supplies. These two groups of Commandos supplied much useful information that assisted the Americans in clearing the island of Japanese. In one instance, Captain Williams and two Fijians crept to within a few feet of a group of Japanese. In another, he was out with three Fijians and suddenly ran into a dozen Japanese, who got the bigger fright and ran for their lives. Evidently the size of the New Zealander had them worried, or they were poorly armed. There was now much sickness in the unit, and the patrols returned to Guadalcanal on 26th September.

Guadalcanal

In the meantime, the rest of the unit on Guadalcanal had been trying to locate some Japanese who had been coming out of their hideouts at night and cutting telephone wires. On 21st September, a stick of bombs straddled the Commandos' camp and seven of their number were seriously wounded. Two of the Japanese planes that were shot down landed among the unit's tents. Wreckage was strewn everywhere and much equipment was damaged. The strength of the First Commandos was now 160 men.

Fiji

On 13th September 1943, 23 reinforcements arrived from Fiji. However, some were hospitalised with malaria that was too severe to treat in camp and eight Fijians returned to Fiji as medically unfit. On 5th October, the unit was ordered to Florida Island and they patrolled regularly there, but Florida had lost its importance by this time, except for the harbour at Tulagi. About the middle of October, half the unit went down with malaria. Lieutenant-General A. A. Vandegrift, Commanding General of the United States Marine Corps in the Pacific, wanted to use at least one platoon of Commandos in his forthcoming attack on Bougainville, but Brigadier Dittmer, who had taken over command of the Fiji Brigade Group, refused to allow the First Commandos to go into action again because of sickness in the unit. It was decided, instead, to send the Second Commandos who were being trained in Fiji.

The First Commandos embarked on 30th November and disembarked at Suva on 11th December. The New Zealanders, who had not had any leave for two years, returned to New Zealand for 28 days' furlough, and the Fijians were granted a similar period of leave in Fiji. When all returned from leave, it was found that three-quarters of them were unfit for further active service, so the First Commando Fiji Guerillas was disbanded on 27th May, 1944. Father was awarded the DSO "For gallant and distinguished services in the South Pacific", announced by the War Office on 17th February 1944. The approval for the award included the following statement:

> While commanding the 1st Commando Fiji Guerillas, which was organised and officered by personnel of 8th Brigade Group, Major Tripp displayed conspicuous gallantry and devotion to duty. During the attack on New

Georgia in 1943 he led his men with great courage and skill. On one occasion, during a night operation, he was attacked at close quarters by two Japanese, one of whom discharged his rifle at short range, the flash burning Major Tripp's arm and chest. He killed both of the Japanese. Though wounded, he continued in command of his unit until it was withdrawn to reorganise.

On 25th June 1944, he was awarded the Silver Star by the Commanding General of the United States Army forces in the South Pacific Area. The citation accompanying the award was as follows:

> Charles W. H Tripp, Major, first Battalion, South Pacific Scouts, for gallantry in action at New Georgia, Solomon Islands, during the period from 6 July to 13 July 1943. Major Tripp commanded a company of South Pacific Scouts and personally led patrols into areas known to contain Japanese pillboxes armed with machine guns. On one occasion, when enemy forces were conducting nightly harassing attacks on an infantry regiment, he took a patrol of his scouts far beyond the front lines, and with patient care and skill patrolled in and out of an enemy bivouac area. Discovered by the Japanese he conducted his men with such dexterity as to draw the enemy's ineffectual fire and thus reveal their definite positions. During this period, Major Tripp, armed with hand grenades, crawled to within a few feet of hostile pillboxes and caused destruction to the enemy. Though completely cut off from the American forces, on one occasion he led his company over dense jungle terrain, and by dusk reached the American lines. There he reported in detail the location of an estimated enemy battalion to the commanding officer of an infantry regiment. The information obtained by his courageous effort contributed in a large measure to the success of the military operations against the enemy forces. By Command of Lieutenant General Harmon.

Interesting information concerning this award is contained in a letter sent by the Governor General of New Zealand on advice from the Prime Minister, Peter Fraser, to the Secretary of State for Dominion Affairs, in which he said:

> Major Tripp has already been recommended for the D.S.O by the High Commissioner for the Western Pacific for his services during the operations in New Georgia, and although the rules governing the acceptance of foreign awards state that it is desirable to avoid duplication

and the grant of a foreign as well as of a British decoration for the same service, it is considered that, in view of the outstanding serviced rendered by Major Tripp, and the fact that he has throughout the operations of the Solomons been closely associated with the United States Forces, the proposed award should, provided the United Kingdom Authorities see no objection, be accepted. Prime Minister would be grateful if proposal could be considered in relation to quota and with a view to acceptance.

Other medals include the 1939-45 Star, the Pacific Star, the Defence Medal, the War Medal 1939-45 and the NZ Service Medal.

The esteem in which Father was held by Fijian Chiefs, troops and dignitaries is evidenced in the whale tooth necklace with which he was presented as Chief in his own right. As late as the early 1980s, because of the respect Fijians had for his ability to instil discipline, he was asked to join the Council of Chiefs in Fiji and discuss the problem of unruly youngsters and methods of correcting the situation.

Back home

One story relating to Father's return to New Zealand is worth telling. One night in Guadalcanal, before he returned to Fiji, there was a bombing raid and an American ammunition dump went up in flames. The Commandos somehow managed to salvage a jeep from the raid, and, as all the records were destroyed, they kept it. When they returned to Fiji Father succeeded in getting the jeep shipped back with them. When in Fiji they had the Commando colours painted on the bonnet. Father was friendly with Katrine Brown, who was head of the WAAFs in Fiji and a very capable lady. They had great respect for one another. He gave her the use of the jeep and she made very good use of it, driving out to remote areas to get eggs and other supplies at a time when rations were short. Because the Commandos were so well known in Fiji, she was welcome anywhere, and the Fijians would rally around when they saw the colours on the jeep and give her what she required. When he returned to New

Zealand Father asked if, when she returned, she would attempt to find a captain of a ship heading for New Zealand, who would be willing to take the jeep on board and deliver it here. Father had spoken to the local policeman in Gore about having it on the farm, and the latter said that as long as he never saw it in Gore he wouldn't report it.

Katrine did find a captain, who said that he would take it the next time he made a trip to Lyttelton. The arrangement was that it would be unloaded off the boat at night and Father would drive it home in the dark. However, when the ship arrived, he was busy (shearing I think), so he arranged for it to be parked in a garage in Christchurch until he could collect it. However, the captain apparently got cold feet and didn't unload it, so the jeep went back to Fiji. Years later Katrine told me that, if she had known Father was not going to be there, she would have come down from the North Island and driven it off herself. She said she never forgave Father for that! I was present at Katrine's funeral in the Christchurch Catholic Cathedral and regretted not having asked the priest conducting the service if I could have told that story. Mother said that when Dad came back from the war he was fitter than she had ever seen him.

Father was once asked how he coped with the war experience and he replied that it was just like one great holiday. However, I believe the war experience affected him very deeply. Rosa, who was closer to Father in his final years, was more aware of this. Some decisions he had to make must have been extraordinarily difficult. Mother told me that he once had a vivid dream in which he saw five of his men killed and saw the circumstances where they lay. It happened later almost exactly as he had dreamt. He told me that on occasion he had the sense he was sending men to their death. He also told me that he had seen men rolling cigarettes which they told him they knew would be their last. He once told me that he was living on borrowed time. Another story Mother told happened one night as they were sleeping together. There must have been a draught, and the bedroom door opened slightly. Father was out of bed in a flash and had one hand on the door handle and the other by his hip where his pistol would have been. He then realised where he was and looked round with a sheepish grin on his face and went back to bed.

One man who was in the Second Commandos told me, a good few years after the war, of one of his own experiences. He was with a group of Fijians not far from base when they realised they had left something behind. He told them to wait where they were and he would run back and get it as quickly as he could. When he returned, he ran into the group and then realised to his horror that they were not Fijians sitting around but Japanese. The Fijians had heard them coming and melted into the bush. He immediately turned around and ran out again. They started shooting, but fortunately only hit his water bottle. He was still having occasional nightmares years later.

My favourite story about Father, told me by a Gore RSA member, occurred after the war, when Freyberg, who was then Governor-General, did a tour of the RSA groups around the country. A parade was held in Gore to which Father turned out with his medals. When Freyberg came down the line he noticed Father's Silver Star and said to him, "Where did you get that? They didn't give many of those away." Father told him he had been in the First Commandos. Freyberg then asked, "Did you know colonel so-and-so?" Father replied, "Yes. He was a bloody idiot." Freyberg looked at him and said, "I would like you to know he was my brother-in-law". He then told Father that he would like to talk to him and would he turn up at five o'clock. Father duly arrived at five and they had drinks together and a good yarn.

One thing that Father learned in the Commandos was how to throw a knife. Ginger told me that several times Father took him out and got him to practise. He said, "One day it may save your life." Ginger said that if Father threw the knife into a macrocarpa it was a job to get it out.

After the war Father became a member of the National Rehabilitation Council, specialising in the settlement of returned servicemen on farms. Remembering back to an unsuccessful scheme after World War 1, he used all his persuasive powers to have the Government of the day make sure that all farms settled under the scheme were sufficient in carrying capacity to withstand future difficult years and inflationary periods. He gave much time to this. He was a regular supporter of the Gore R.S.A., being President 1949-50. During the war, and for years after, the R.S.A. received a cattle beast for welfare.

Further thoughts about my Father

Father was one of nature's gentlemen. He would always insist that I go through a door ahead of him. I wouldn't argue with that. He had great powers of observation and very good eyesight up until the day he died. The night before he died, Ginger visited him in the Gore hospital. Father was making a minor adjustment to his hearing aid. Ginger offered to help him with it. Father's comment was, "You wouldn't be able to see it without your glasses." He must have had a near photographic memory. Kipling was his favourite poet. He told me that in his younger days he could read a poem of Kipling's and then quote it straight off. I remember Jonathan Elworthy telling me that he travelled once from Timaru to Dunedin (it may have been Christchurch to Timaru, but I think it was Timaru to Dunedin) with Father and someone else. He said that Father kept them entertained by quoting Kipling's poems all the way. Ginger once told me that Dad could remember everything he had read. He must have had some poetic skills himself, as the following poem of his is quoted by Mother in her booklet *Memories of Charlie W. H. Tripp*. He wrote it when about 14, after a holiday at Orari Gorge, and sent it to Granny Ellen Tripp instead of writing a thank you letter.

I tried, I tried and tried again,
and nearly strained my little brain,
but all my efforts were in vain
to make a rhyme.
Where is it that the rabbits flee,
on seeing harmless little me,
where is it that I long to be,
Orari Gorge.
Where is it that the wild pigs roam,
when I stalk them all alone,
where I would sooner be than home,
Orari Gorge.
Where is it that I chance to see,
Miss Islip hide the storeroom key,
where was the feed I got so free,
Orari Gorge.
Where is that much beloved tin shanty,
with many tasties in the pantry,
where is the house that's bossed by Aunty,
Orari Gorge
What though I to a hundred be
and live on either land or sea,
yet always in my dreams I see,
Orari Gorge

Father had one gift that few knew about, and which he didn't develop. We have a framed drawing of the Christ's College chapel on the wall of our hallway. It wasn't until my teen years that I realised it was drawn by my father. He told us that he used to draw things under the desk during classes at school and sell them for 10 shillings. Rosa has several other framed drawings from those days, which show he had considerable talent in that area.

One of Father's major interests was the Scouting Movement. In 1986, the Scouting Movement of New Zealand awarded him the

Medal of Merit 'for good services to the Scout Movement'. It is worth recording the accompanying citation:

> There are no records available locally to tell us what position Mr Tripp held prior to 1948, but it is believed that he did hold a warrant as a Scout leader.
>
> From 1948 to 1958 he held the position of District Chairman and District Secretary, and since 1958 has been the Patron of the District.
>
> Mr Tripp has a tremendous interest in, and a very high regard for, the Scouting Movement, and although now in his 80th year, still attends the District Annual Meeting and Dinner, accompanied by Mrs Tripp.
>
> One of his aims has been to ensure that as many boys as possible have the opportunity of becoming a Scout, and to this end he contributes yearly to District funds with a substantial donation.
>
> It is a well-known fact that his work in the field is done with no thought of public recognition.
>
> It therefore gives His Excellency the Governor General, in his capacity as Chief Scout of New Zealand, the greatest pleasure in awarding Charles W. Tripp further recognition by way of the Medal of Merit. His services were honoured in 1964, when he received the Chief Scout Commendation.
>
> Signed: L. E. Williams, Area Commissioner.

Appendix

From The Daily Telegraph, Second Book of Obituaries; Heroes and Adventurers, edited by Hugh Massingberd, printed 1991, reprinted 1997. This chapter used by permission of The Daily Telegraph.

LT-COL CHARLES "THE BOSS" TRIPP

Lieutenant-Colonel Charles "The Boss" Tripp, who has died aged 89, achieved notable successes in command of the 1st Commando Fiji Guerrillas when operating behind Japanese lines in the southern island group between late 1942 and late 1943.

When the unit was eventually disbanded in May 1944, 40% of the officers and 30% of the sergeants had been killed in action behind enemy lines.

In December 1942, although Japanese expansion to the south and the immediate threat to Australia had been checked by the Battle of the Coral Sea, the Japanese still occupied every island of tactical value in the south-west Pacific. General MacArthur's strategy was to recapture key bases in a series of hopping movements until he reached Iwo Jima and Okinawa—and an invasion on Japan itself became practical.

But the Japanese were building an airfield on Guadalcanal and a seaplane base at Tulagi. They would put up a determined opposition to any Allied invasion force as they had massed their troops for the further attempt on Australia.

In order to operate in the Japanese rear areas and acquire intelligence, a 200-strong Commando force was raised; it contained New Zealanders, English, Americans, and a mixture of Fijians, Tongans and Solomon Islanders. Although already 40, Tripp was the toughest and most enduring man in the unit, as well as being an inspired leader who earned the affectionate sobriquet of "The Boss".

A New Zealander, Charles William Howard Tripp was born on February 22 1902, and educated at Christ's College, Christchurch, New Zealand, and Trinity Hall, Cambridge. On leaving the university he returned to New Zealand where he first worked at Orari Gorge which was settled by his grandfather in 1855. Later, he bought Nithdale in Southland.

When he volunteered for the Army at the start of the Second World War he was graded as being too old; in an attempt to keep him out of harm, he was posted to Fiji. When the Commando unit was formed, missionaries, who had spent 40 years damping down the Fijians' warlike instincts, we now called on for advice on rekindling it, which they supplied. Recruiting was carried out with regard to native customs, which included quaffing numerous bowls of *Kava* and the presentation of whale's teeth to the officers.

By the time the Commandos were ready for action, rigorous training schedules had made them expert in bushcraft, camouflage, jungle warfare and silent killing.

Their first successful operation was on Guadalcanal, where they dislocated Japanese plans, inflicted numerous casualties and acquired valuable intelligence on enemy movements and equipment. Up until this time they were known as the Southern Independent Commando, but now Tripp was told to raise a special force to be known as the 1st Commando Fiji Guerillas.

This outfit reached unprecedented heights of marksmanship and jungle warfare endurance. It was said: "When the Fiji Commandos raid at night, death wears velvet gloves."

Communication with the Fijians was in pidgin English; an aircraft was "schooner-belong-Jesus-Christ", but they soon learned to recognise various types, such as B17 and P38.

Initially they used Thompson sub-machine guns, but then found the Australian Owen guns more effective. Much of their work consisted of eliminating the groups of spies that the Japanese had left behind.

Their most important achievement was assisting in the capture of Munda Airfield on New Georgia, around which there were known to be 5,000 Japanese. Tripp's guerrillas arrived after an 11-hour voyage on an American destroyer which was chased by, but escaped from, three Japanese warships. Then they cleared the smaller islands of Japanese before moving inland. The ensuing conflict included numerous close-quarter fights at night. It was described as "very personal".

On one occasion, a Japanese machine-gunner opened up on Tripp, who was leading a patrol, at 10 yards range. Tripp's carbine jammed as he tried to return the fire so he threw the weapon at the gunner and raced off into the undergrowth at what he described as world record-breaking speed. The Japanese threw grenades after him but as he looked for a hiding place he saw another party of a dozen Japanese approaching. He shot the leader with his automatic, and in the confusion managed to slip away and rejoin his patrol.

They settled down for the night only to find they were in the middle of a strongly held enemy position. Inevitably they were discovered, but again managed to escape into the jungle after a brisk fight in the dark.

Tripp had a luckly escape when a Japanese bullet was deflected by his cigarette-lighter—subsequently a Tripp family treasure. When the moon came up, American artillery began shelling the area and Tripp, realising that he could easily be mistaken in the dark for a Japanese, decided to walk around the position while the soldiers were all securely in their foxholes.

In doing so he found various telephone lines to mortar posts, which he cut; their exhausted crews were asleep and he was undetected. He then headed south through a swamp, reached an American regimental HQ and gave them the information he had gathered. In consequence the Americans were able to push on to the coast and secure the beach-head at Laiana.

After the capture of Munda, Tripp took a force of 50 guerillas to Vella Lavelle, where they acquired maps from dead Japanese and identified various targets for American artillery. This prevented the Japanese from turning the island into a strongpoint.

At the conclusion of these exploits, Tripp was awarded the DSO and the American Silver Star. Thirty-five other members of his guerillas received gallantry awards.

Tripp's citation mentioned that "the 1st Commando Fiji Guerrillas furnished distant reconnaissance patrols which worked well into enemy territory often at great hazard and furnished battle guides, and in some instances actually led front-line units in combat and assaults on enemy positions. Tripp himself engaged in much patrolling in addition to planning, supervising and conducting the activities of the entire detachment in a most capable fashion".

He later described his guerrilla work as "the best three years' holiday I had ever had, and I got paid for it too". After the war he was involved in the rehabilitation of ex-Servicemen and land allocations.

Tripp was noted for his pioneering spirit and his readiness to embrace all the technological advances in agriculture. Both Baden-Powell and Shackleton stayed with the family and from these visits Tripp became extremely interested in pioneering and Antarctica; he eventually assembled one of the largest collections of Antarctic memorabilia in the Southern Hemisphere.

At Cambridge he had been a respectable oarsman and a good boxer and rugby footballer, as well as acquiring a lifelong passion for Kipling which he could recite for hours on end.

Back in New Zealand he became a world-renowned cattle breeder and exported many Poll Herefords to Canada and Britain where they won prizes and record prices. "The Boss" was a tall, taciturn, raw-boned figure who believed in leading from the front and trusting his men. Very few failed him.

An altogether exceptional man, Charles Tripp had sailed around Cape Horn twice before he was 10 and was still getting up a 5am in the month he died in his 90th year.

His wife, Myra, passed on before him. They had three sons and two daughters.

About the Author

My parents were an exceptional couple. Their characters and their influence in the local community, the farming world and in a much wider sphere were significant. Father's contribution to the war effort in the Solomon Islands well deserved the Silver Star given him by the Americans—this story is unique and is one that you will not find in many of the war histories. I was too young during the war to really appreciate this. Mother, too, well deserved the QSM she received for her work in the community. These stories deserve to be told, and I have valued the opportunity to pass them on to present and future generations of the family and others who may be interested.

Father did not often speak about the war, but every so often, when we were out together, he would come up with personal stories. These I remember in vivid detail. I believe it is these stories, told by him, or by others who knew him, that give life to the events and more than anything else reveal his character.

We are all greatly influenced, for better or worse, by those we are closest to in our youth, and I have always been thankful for the parents God gave me, both in the personal example they set me and the opportunities they provided for me. For whatever interest it may have for my descendants, I have also decided to include here some additional youthful experiences that have significantly influenced my own life's journey and the goals and values that have moulded who I am.

I became a Christian around the age of sixteen, while a student at Christ's College. We had a visit to the school one evening by a preacher from England who had been invited by the Crusader Movement, now the Scripture Union. He explained the basics of the Christian faith, of which, up to that time, I knew little about. However, what he said made sense and that night I made a commitment of my life to Jesus, a decision that was to colour all my future.

When I was 19, my father sent me overseas to Cambridge University to study agriculture. In some respects, I was rather immature, but in those days I did what I was told! Agriculture only lasted for three weeks as I decided that people mattered more to me than animals, so I studied medicine for a year before changing to theology.

What meant most to me during those years was not so much the experience of Cambridge itself, but having the chance to know people who were to significantly influence my understanding of the Christian faith. There are two to whom I particularly owe a great deal. The first was Michael Perrott, a student at Trinity Hall who was leading the Christian Union in the College at that time. He was a year ahead of me and took me under his wing when I arrived and later invited me to stay with him in Dublin during a semester. We keep in touch.

The second was Rev. John Stott, one of the most influential Christian leaders of the last generation. I had the privilege of meeting him on several occasions. His preaching, books and personal encouragement provided me with a wonderful grounding in understanding the Bible. This was invaluable to me when I began writing booklets and books on the Christian faith, on retirement from active ministry[1].

I also gained much from being able to take part in Christian Conferences, student missions and beach missions run by the Children's Special Service Mission, and played a small part in the Billy Graham three month crusade in Harringay Arena in London and a week in Cambridge where he preached nightly in the University Church.

On returning to New Zealand, after two years in Theological College I was ordained into the Anglican ministry and spent most of that ministry in parishes around Christchurch, including six years in a country parish.

Dick Tripp

---

[1] For those who may wish to know more about my spiritual journey and what it has meant to me, go to www.christianity.co.nz and click on the link 'The Author' where I have described it in some detail. The website contains the full text of all the books and booklets I have written, which can be downloaded free as pdf files from the website or eBooks from iTunes.

www.ingramcontent.com/pod-product-compliance
Lightning Source LLC
Chambersburg PA
CBHW051410290426
44108CB00015B/2224